AF265998

I CAN DEPEND ON GOD

Straight from the heart

By

Destiny Roane

© 2003 by Destiny Roane. All rights reserved.

No part of this book may be reproduced, stored in a
retrieval system, or transmitted by any means,
electronic, mechanical, photocopying, recording, or
otherwise, without written permission from the author.

ISBN: 1-4107-7894-0 (e-book)
ISBN: 1-4107-7893-2 (Paperback)

This book is printed on acid free paper.

1stBooks – rev. 10/23/03

Since I have developed a personal relationship with Jesus Christ, I have learned to lean and depend on Him. Jesus is my presence help in the time of joy and sorrow. Jesus is my hope for yesterday, today, and tomorrow. Jesus is the giver of peace, love, joy, life of abundance, and a lot more. Why should you be lack of anything, when God has everything? Because my Father is rich, you can also be rich with blessings.

Dedications:

I give thanks unto my Lord Jesus Christ for blessing and allowing me to write of His goodness and love.

I thank my belated parents, Bishop Roane and Thelma Rea Roane, for teaching God's word. The time-shared and enduring patience meant so much to me. Because of your prayers, teachings, and love for God, I began to eventually get my life in prospective with God's word. Mom would always say to me, "Girl, if you don't use your talent, Jesus will give the gift of writing to someone else. Whenever you are blessed with a gift, you should use it to God's glory." Thanks for answering my questions on salvation, peace, prayer, and how can one be assured of his/her calling?

I thank my oldest sister (Rea Unique) who recognized my gift and encouraged me to continue writing. I am thankful for my brothers and sisters, and I say to them to aim high and set higher goals. As dad quoted, "Seek ye first the kingdom of God and other things will be added unto you."

I thank all of the Christian mothers, fathers, brothers, sisters, and friends who helped to encourage me to do the work of Jesus Christ. May God continue to bless you, you, and you?

I would love to see more year-around programs that assist the children in mathematics and reading skills; as well as, activities in a variety of sports and musical instruments. We must make these programs affordable and offer grants so that the children that are in need are not left out. Children have too much idle time on their hands; therefore, we must give the children hope, a better future, and a positive outcome. We must save the children from violence, drug abuse, alcohol abuse, running away, homeless, and school dropouts. Children are not only a part of the future; children are vital today. I trust that God is about to begin a work in me; the purpose and focus of this task is to help the children to grow and be intellectual, spiritual, and valuable within our churches, schools, and communities. We must start helping the children before it is too late.

Table of Contents:

Fruit of the Spirit—Love

Love is God's first commandment to mankind
His love is pure and it is also divine
I questioned God's love and this is what I find

Love was formed at the beginning of creation
And love will stand at the end
Love bears all things with an understanding
That fulfills my heart and no emptiness exists.

The feeling of love gives enjoyment and happiness
Love is purer than shining gold
It cannot be brought nor is it sold
Love can transform the human mind
Love taught me to be sweet and kind
It cannot be replace
With materialist things
True love is real and pure.

Love has conquered my fears
Love is feeling God's presence near
In my heart I hold much treasure
A love that unique and genuine
Is never forsaken and
It cannot be mistaken.

I realize love is God most precious gift.

Comfort With Peace

Peace is a harmonious relation
Between God, others, and myself
The inner contentment that dwell
And witness the Spirit of righteous within.

Peace is calmness
Yet it shows patience, love, and serenity
To follow peace means
Goodness, mercy, and grace
To believers seeking God face.

Peace is a state of tranquility
When the storm of life is ragging
Trouble cannot disturb
Nor take away thy joy
Because the peace of God
Give thee comfort and assurance.

Peace makes me to stand still
And see the wondrous and marvelous work
That's in the Master's will.

I am blessed to be a servant
Covered by Jesus' blood
His blood shall never its lose power
But will save, shield, and
Protect thee from evil and harm.

The Omnipotent

Lord, I am here praying
And I don't know what to say
In your presence alone I stand
Stretching forth my hands.

There's something within me
That I cannot explain
It also heals the pain
And will not let me go astray.

In thy Word I shall abide
And my sins I cannot hide
Please purify my body, soul, and mind
In the Word I find
The guidance to how I should live.

I still cannot explain
What is happening to me?

Lord, I know you understand.

Faith

Faith is being steadfast
Abiding in the Word of God
Because God spoken it
It shall come to pass
That is the reason why?
I trust and believe.

Faith is a substance of hope
Even though I cannot see it
I can feel it is about to happen
Because God has promised
That is the reason why?
I wait patiently to receive.

Faith can unlock closed doors
It also moves mountains
Prayer is the key that fits, and
God opens the door wide
To allow you to enter inn
You must be in the spirit because
The natural eyes cannot see it.

Without faith and works
It is impossible to please God.

Destiny Roane

The House

Except the Lord build the house
The builder labor is in vain
The house must be built on God's word
So the enemy cannot destroy it by hand.

The house made from bricks
Will eventually fall down
The strong wind will blow it away
The stormy sea chasten it by the flood
Because it was built upon the sand and
The house built by man can be destroyed.

Hear my prayer dear Lord
Please purge and prepare me
A house where love and peace abide
Rooted and grounded in God's word
Built upon a foundation that strong
And if the Devil should prevail
My soul is anchored in the Lord
And I am washed in Jesus blood.

The word of God shall forever stand.
Heaven and earth shall both pass away
So build your affections on heavenly gain.

Destiny Roane

In The Beginning

From the dust God created Adam
Since man should not be alone
God made Adam to fall into a deep sleep
From Adam's rib was taken a bone
And God placed this rib
Into a woman named Eve
Eve became Adam's helpmate
And no one knows how this was done?

We were created to do God's will
Satan comes to steal and to kill
And attempt the flesh to lust
In the Lord I will always trust.

Listen attentively with your ears
The Lord is truly near
God's word brings joy that fulfills.

God's love works no man ill
Jesus will fight your battle
If you just only keep still.

Hate is Destructive

What causes man to hate?
A lever-old man named the devil
And if you are not careful
He will slip evil on you.

The devil walks upon the earth
Seeking whom He may destroy
Be not defeated by Satan
Neither be destroyed by hate because
Jesus stands and patiently waits
At the door of your heart
Wont you open up your heart
And allow Jesus to come in.

God is a man of color
He is the Lord and Savior
I rejoice and give God the glory
And one day I'll tell my story.

Anchor In The Lord

The hands of the Lord anoints
With the power and authority God appoints.

In thy Word, I am approved,
By faith my mountains shall be moved.

God's word my heart believe,
And the Holy Spirit I receive.

Weeping for a while may endure,
But peace and comfort I can assure.

My salvation in Christ is zeal
Through prayer my answer is revealed
My name in the Holy Book is sealed.

I Can Depend on God

I called upon the Lord in distress
He answered me in a soft voice
Saying be strong in the liberty
Whereby I set you free of captivity
In my heart, I will keep God's word
When the enemy shall prevail,
I will have thy word for my sword.

Lord let me not be ashamed
To give praises to you for delivering me
It was at the cross where
Jesus died without sin or blame
Still the love for mankind has not changed.

In Despair

Although the storm of life is a fight
God, Most high, is powerful and mighty
In despair, the Lord is near
His perfect love casts out fear
Jesus made great light
The moon and stars to rule by night
His word of truth is upright
Be patient, while waiting to hear
What the Savior has to say
Jesus gives hope and eternal life
To obey thy word is my desire and delight.

Destiny Roane

The Importance of Prayer

Men ought to always pray
Or he will get weak along the way
Abiding in God's word
Keeps him from going astray
Purifying his mind and thoughts every day
Keeps thy mind from becoming cloudy and gray
Joy, peace, kindness, and love
Jesus will put into the heart.

If you're strong and rooted
In God's word
It isn't easy for the adversary to attempt
Nor mold you like clay
Don't let the time of our Savior coming
Find thee unprepared or
Engaged in a worldly act
Be strong my brother and my sister
Because the end of time is drawing
Near to judgment day.

Father's Blessings

Father instructs love ones and teaches
With wisdom he guides and directs
He speaks in love and respect
The unspoken words reflect his life
That he lives by what he preaches.

Father works and keeps the family together
He labor through cold and hot weather
To keep everything in line
He ensures the family great support.

Mother's Blessings

A mother has a special love
That God gives her from above
Granted with serenity, wisdom, and grace
Encourages a child to do right instead of wrong
Her patience endures many hours
She patiently instructs the love ones
How to be self-confidence and strong?
In all that you do be not dismay
Jesus is there to help you in every way.

26

Mother

Because mother cares and understands,
She is always there to lend a helping hand
To achieve and succeed life demand,
She gave me hope to take a stand
And to follow life dream is my command.

As I look over my life
Putting faith into great stride
With the knowledge that I was taught
And self-determination toward my goals
I will eventually derive.

In The Valley, Is Where Trouble Rises

In the depth of the valley, I cried
Because the cross that I had to carry
Seemed impossible and heavy to bear
My mind was beginning to get weary
And I wondered if I had
Lost my way from the right path.

When my strength was weakened
And about to fail,
Then the Lord increased my faith
And revived my soul.

In the depth of the valley,
My soul felt forsaken
And like a prisoner cast in jail
Down on my knees
I had to stay and tarry
I waited patiently for Jesus to stop by
Deliverance and power came into the midst
Jesus unlatched the chains
Rescued me and paid my bail.

Dear Heavenly Father

Most gracious and Heavenly Father I pray
Who sees, knows, and hears
The words I am about to say
The awesome of life's burdens
And problems cause us to weary or fear
Sometimes bring sorrow and often
We shed tears
There is nothing that could harm your children
Thus, we are forever in Jesus care.

God is our refuge and protection.
He will renew our strength each day
His work is wondrous, powerful, and might
Thy word of truth shines through
Darkness and light
May my life be pleasing because
The Lord's way is sweet and right
Jesus, the only begotten Son of God,
Is the everlasting life.

Jesus and I

Jesus heard me praying
He stood right by my side
In this troubled world,
The lord never left me alone
I said, Lord don't let the water
Roll me up with the tide.

The Lord was watching over me
When I ran out on the water,
The water was cold
The water chilled my body
My soul remained warm.

Then the Lord said to me,
I am with you child
Not just part of the way
Not just the beginning but until the end.

Your name is in the book of life.
Just keep praising my name
And don't feel ashamed of lifting
Up holy hands unto the Lord
Which is on high.

I felt so happy
I didn't know what to do
I prayed all day Saturday, and
I went to church on Sunday
On Monday I received my blessing

Destiny Roane

A saint came to me
And begin praising the Lord with me
It made my soul happy
And certainly it made me rejoice
For serving the Lord
Will pay off after while.

A Voice From Above

God spoke to me last night
His voice was tender and sweet
Then the clouds began to clear up
The dark shadows in the sky.

I begin to hear His voice
Which was coming from above
Jesus said to me,
There is no other way and
You must come in at the door.

Once your heart is right
Help to bring one or two more souls
Turn away from their sinful ways
God said to me,
This is not the end of time
There shall be more
To seek to be born again
Cause up here is nothing but salvation
But down on earth
You shall witness to what
Is the book of Revelation?

The holy Bible is true
So consider my child today
Don't put off for tomorrow
What you can do today.

Hell has enlarged
For the devil and his angels
And if your heart is not right
Your soul will be lost.

Consider today where
You want to spent eternity
And what will happen to your soul.
If you don't come this way?

Accepting the Call

Having accepted the call
Laboring strongly in the faith
Spreading God's word to all
Surely comfort and peace
I have found
Knowing the seed fell on good ground.

The youths are called to be strong
The elders are blessed with wisdom
And together we can all
Enter into God's kingdom.

After this work on earth is done
God will judge the wrong
And at last…
Victory will be won.

Our Hope And Dream

To teach our youths to survive
And keep their hope alive
Mean reaching high to achieve
With an open mind and heart to believe.

The Lord will help us to survive
He will renew our spirit
Eternal life Jesus will give
And the best gift you can receive
Is the gift of everlasting life?

Unity

Unity brings strength
To our family, body of Christ, and nation
The adversary cannot easily enter
And problems won't linger near.

Spiritual power within is endured
The prayers and praises are assured
The spiritual connection is pure.

Unity is rooted in love, and
Granted with empowerment from above
We cast our burdens upon the Lord
Knowing we shall be sustained
Because God will never suffer
The righteous to be moved.

Unity works togetherness
Allowing true believers to assembly and agree
And stay on the same accordance
Being committed unto the Lord
Our work and thoughts will be established
When we seek the Heavenly Father for
Help of his countenance.

Unity makes us steadfast
And always bounded in the Word of God.

There's No Escape

The last enemy called death
Take away our breath
Then a host of angels shall carry
The soul to the other side
I leave my work behind that says
I've kept the faith and fought a good fight

Jesus shall appear with great might
Around the world shines bright light
And our Lord arriving
What a glory sight
God's word still stands
And Satan works has finally past.

God Is Always There

The Lord is always near, and
He listens with a tender ear
Sometimes the cross becomes heavy to bear
When toils face us unaware
Often we cannot understand
Why life bear aches and pains?

God's goodness and mercy still sustain
He holds the world in His hands
One day we will go back with Him
To that promised land
Where the angels rejoice over a warrior
Whose work on earth successfully done
And victory in Christ truly won.

I Am Blessed

I am blessed with abundance
That gold and silver cannot buy
With health, family and friends
And I'm happy just being alive.

I am blessed with abundance
It doesn't trouble my mind
A divine inspiration, peace, and wisdom
It adds strength to my spirit growth.

I am blessed with abundance
It is not measured by possession
But I'm trusting in the Lord
Who promised to supply all of my needs?

At the Throne of God

I took a moment to look within
And experience the Holy Spirit
I felt the anointing of God's peace
Flowing through my mind and soul
Harmony and love took its course
For all my worries were left behind.

At the throne of God
A new change has come over me
I found love, joy, and peace
At the fountain springs living water
That quenched my thirst
The water is the God's word
The plan of salvation that given
To everyone who believe in Jesus Christ.

Now I am accepting new challenges and
Seeking the truth in the good
I am determine to walk in the likeness
Of the Almighty God.

Let Your Joy Be Full

Joy is overcoming trials
Without putting up a fight
But praying to the Lord
Who is mighty and powerful?

Joy is receiving many blessings
And when my cup is overflowing
Blessings cannot be counted or measured
All I know is joy gives me excitement

These blessings are from my Heavenly Father
Which brings me joy and
Joy is contentment and happiness.
Jesus said, my joy I give you
It is a feeling deep in my soul
And it cannot be disturbed
Therefore, I have peace
That is also my joy.

52

No Other Like Him

53

My Savior was crucified upon the cross
Without a cause nor blame
Jesus arms were stretched wide
With piercing arrows in His sides
He did not mine dying
So that we may live
There's no excuse for me to sin because
Cause Jesus died to set us free.

A Winning Christian

To increase your faith and
Strength your spiritual growth
God's word will teach you how
To be not defeated but overcome
Trials and temptations
You can count it all joy
When you overcome evil with good.

When the flesh gets weak
And your spirit sometimes become low
Stay content in God's word
Holding onto what you already know.

Job's Suffering

57

Job was a righteous man
Tested on every hand
Yet he stood every test
And continue to give God His best
At last Job was truly blessed.

The Hour Is Come

No man knows not the day nor hour
Our Savior shall appear
He may come back
Like a thief in the night
Keep your lamp trimmed with light
And your heart always rights.

Life of Abundance

Although the righteous suffer
With grief and pain
I set my hope above earthly gain
I share happiness in sunshine or rain
Because God's goodness and mercy
Shall be with me.

Salvation Is Deliverance

Salvation is the deliverance
And grace by which the soul is saved
From danger, evil and damnation.

The Holy Spirit now resides within
Thus, the power of salvation overcome our sins
We are given a second chance
To get our life priorities in order
And an opportunity to inherit
The kingdom of God
It's a believer renewing
Spiritual birth.

The mind, body, and soul
Are delivered from ailment
It set the bound free
It opens the blind eyes
It opens the dumb mouth
It gives limbs to the cripple
Then the power of Salvation moves upon
Man's heart to carry out God's plan.

Salvation demonstrates the truth
That shines in the light
The escape of sickness and death
Is man last fighting enemy, but
It is the best part of God's plan.

Destiny Roane

Salvation prepares God's saints for everlasting life
The works of Jesus, Christ
I find it wonderful and marvelous
Salvation helps to discipline us
When we are act or get out of place
It directs us back on the right track.

(CONTINUED)

Life of Abundance

There is none righteous
No not one!
We can all follow Jesus
Perfect example.

God's Word is...

The word is light
Darkness comphrend it not

The word is joy
Let thee joy be full.

Joy of the flowing rivers that
Make my cup overflow.

The word is salvation
It saves my soul from hell

The word is powerful
It cuts deeper than a sword
It also suppress my memory and
Thoughts that are in my mind.

The word is security
It protects me from harm
It keeps me in perfect
Peace until Jesus returns.

The word is justice
Obey God's commandment and
Keep His word.

These are my testimonies of the word
I seek and ask God for wisdom, knowledge
And understanding of the
Master's plan.

Yield Not to Satan

Satan needs only an inch
To enter anyone's life
Satan will slide in
And take full control
He comes to steal, kill, and destroy.

Once Satan given an invitation
There is no peace to be found
He does not discriminate
Gender, color, nor age
He will accept you
As you are
And your life will be an outrage.

Satan does not stop
At an inch, yard, nor mile
His job is to become a Prince that rules.

Satan of principalities and
Evil spreading into dark places
He is putting in double time
He never takes a day off
Nor a holiday
Nor a vacation
Nor does he sleeps
Because Satan knows
The rapture is drawing near.

Patience

Jesus' spirit manifest patience
And love with meekness
He became human
And identified himself to man
When he walked upon the earth
He spread the word of God
The miracles followed deliverance
And bear witness
That he is the Son of God
Fulfilling the Father's work
The disciples and others Jesus taught
To call your enemies' name in prayer
Always pray to the Father, which is in Heaven
And have a heart to forgive
Because that is the righteous way
Christians ought to live.

Jesus' patience endures longsuffering
Without bitterness nor a complaint
His kindness and passion for humanity
Allowed Jesus to take a stand
And carryout God, the Father's will
He was crucified on the cross
For the sins of the world
Jesus cried to the Father
I commit my spirit
Into the Father's hands.

Therefore patience eases my pain
When I face difficult times
I don't worry nor fret; for
I shall compass peace and
Inherit a heavenly gain
I take heed to God's word
And I am ever so careful
To render good and not evil
And if it meant suffering
For Jesus, Christ

(Continued)

Patience

I shall be blessed by God, and
It is a good cause.

Jesus waits diligently with patience
He allows us time to change
He stands at your heart and waits
For you to let Him in.

The Evil versus Good Tongue

The tongue that speaks evil
Life is shadowed by darkness
Carrying out no good deeds because
It bears Satan's seed.

The road of destruction
Draw a large crowd because of
The desires for a glamour life style
With fortunes and shining gold.

Yet no joy and peace is found
Cast down and out of the safety zone
Is when you come to your right mind?
Satan has almost sold you out.

It is now time to surrender
Jesus has given you another chance
And ordered Satan to let you go.

The Good Tongue

The tongue that speaks of good deeds
Realize and acknowledge there is a God
The tongue speaks truth and knowledge
Bearing witness Jesus is life.

When seeking peace with fellowman
This tongue fulfills a good work
The heavenly Father dwell and
In the midst of God's presence
There is joy, serenity, and tranquility.

Tongue Speaking Began...

The people of God were on one accord
They freely uttered the preached
Word and truth
At the harvest feast called Pentecost
When a sudden mighty wind of
God's presence filled the upper room.

God heard the people prayers
And knew their heart desire
Then His spirit rested on each one
Who was praying in that room?
Fell upon clover tongues of fire.

From that sacred moment
Believers went into the street
Worshiping in Jesus' name
The crowd listening were amazed
Of the different languages called Tongue.

Men from Arabia, Egypt, and Rome
All tried to explain.
How the Holy Spirit filled the believers?
As Prophet Joel prophesied
God arisen Jesus from the dead
And they were witnesses to the resurrection.

Peter, one of the disciples
Answered the puzzling crowd
This is a sign to the world
Jesus, Christ reign and
Jesus is Truth.

Repent and ye shall receive
This gift of the Holy Spirit, too
Call on Jesus
He still can be found
Open the door
He stands and knocks
Wont you let the Spirit of God come in?

God Cannot

God cannot lie!
God is a spirit and truth
The truth bears witness of God
Which art in Heaven
Jesus the giver of all things
Is the everlasting life?
Ye must serve Him in Spirit and in truth.

God cannot fail!
His word shall not return void
In the beginning was God's word
In the end
The word shall still stand
Jesus did not fail God yet
God gave His only begotten son
To die on the cross
Jesus cried unto the Father
It is finished!

God cannot change!
He is the same
Yesterday, today, and forevermore
God is love and love is God
God's love understand all things
It also casts out fear
It bears all things
And witness the Holy Spirit
So let man be a liar for
God's word is truth.

The truth set the bondage free
It opens the blind eyes
That you may see
It opens the deaf ears
So that you may know and hear
God's word shall forever stand
What He promised?
He will also do.
God cannot lie, change, nor fail!

Judging Before Judgment

Judge not thy brother or sister
To pass judgment is an opinion
And it may not be kind
Nor it may not be the truth
My position is not to judge
God is the judge of both living and death
One day He will judge the right and wrong.

Judging affect others
Especially when it is a deformation
Of anyone's intelligence and character
Don't look to find faults
Don't hold your brother and sister down
By your words and actions
What you are doing says a lot about you?

Judge not and be not judged
Be not a cure or work evil to no man
If you wound God's believers
You have also hurt God
What you did to the least,
You did it also to God?

Before casting a judgment
Take time to think about the Creator
We are created to worship
Jesus, Christ our King
And praises shall forever

Be joyful in thy heart and
Utter from the lips
That the work of God shall go forth.

God shall judge the righteous
According to their work
God shall judge the evildoers
By their iniquities
Don't let the day of our Lord
Find you unprepared or work not done.

Judgment

Judgment is the final trial
Of all mankind
It is the day when Jesus
Shall crack the sky
If your are right, then
It shall be a glory sight
He will come like a theft in the night
May your lamps be trimmed with oil and light?

Judgment is an experience
Jesus, the Son of God endured
To inflict much suffering and punishment
Jesus was persecuted, wounded, and beaten
He was crucified upon the cross
So you and I can be saved
And given the right to the tree of life

It is not God's will for any man to perish
He gave us a choice to decide
Whom we will serve
Would it God or
Would it be Satan?

This time now shall be no more
It is praying time
It is time to start living right
To purge yourself from any sins in your life
To get your heart and house in order

Start by straighten up the mess
So God can come in and truly bless
God will restore what Satan has destroyed?
Jesus shall return and the rewards in His hands.

What Time Is It?

Time is a measurement used by man
To count seconds, hours, days, and weeks
That gradually moves into years
Of decades, events or generations of a lifetime
How do I question time?

Time is a season
Time can never be rolled back
It continues to move forward
It is time for the People to make haste
To value time wisely
And take not another moment to waste
Jesus is still allowing us time
Yet the world is full of darkness
And tribulations come far and near
Jesus is speaking
But the people won't open their ears
Nor recognize God's presence near.

It is time to give God reverence
Now it is high time
For man to awaken out of sleep
And began to sow good seeds
Because what we have sow
We will also reap.

Destiny Roane

Now is time for salvation
To seek God while He is near
And will deliver us from darkness and fear
Jesus is waiting with listening ears
For you call out His name.

Don't let time past by
The tunnel is a dead end
There is no where to run
There is no where to hide
Time is running out.

Music In The Air

God of the universe is almighty
He holds the world in His hand
As I look toward heaven,
I hear music in the air
The clouds are moving in its heavenly place
The birds are flying freely in the sky
The sun appears at the break of dawn
And the moon peaks in the night
What a beautiful sight
There are Hundreds of stars shining bright?

The thunder sometime roars
The sea rolls a tide
The works of God is awesome
He has control over the land and sea
He has power over you and me.

As I look toward the sky
I listen to God speak in
The wind that cometh from the east,
West, north and south
The trees move from side to side
Jesus' name is Hallow in Heaven and earth.

I take heed to God speak
God opens heaven's window and shower blessings
The rain descends from heaven
Even the crops are nurtured in the soil
God sends the snow to purify the earth
And the air we breathe
God's work is marvelous.

Prayer

Prayer is the answer
To every problem and situation
I meditate on God's word
And allow Him to speak into my ears
Thy word reaches the marrow of the bones
It takes a strong hold on me.

Prayer is praise
I thank you Lord for deliverance
For cleanse me from all unrighteousness.

Prayer is repentance
Lord I am sorry for shortcomings
Help me to overcome any temptations
And to get my mind, body, and soul
Focus on Jesus.

Prayer is acknowledging
That I am not all what
I should be, but Lord
Help me to be a doer of thy word.

Prayer is yielding to the Lord.
Lord teach me to be submissive
And allow the Holy Spirit to work on me.
Father, I pray thy will be done
Bless me and find favor.

Prayer extends an openness of heart
Unto our father in Haven
I usher the Holy Spirit
To come into my presence
Lord help me understand
To know my purpose and reason
Manifest in due season
The calling on my life.

Forgiven Is A Must

We must learn to forgive
Ending hatred and begin to live
Respect and love is the greatest gift to give
And in your heart there will be peace.

Don't allow the hurt and pain
To rob you of the unspeakable joy
When nurturing and healing is your gain.

Let your eyes see some good
Give encouragement to others
Be content in God's word and
Don't focus on what has gone wrong
But build your confidence to be strong.

Prayer works every time
No matter if the
Problem great or small
Give it to the Lord
And God will work it out
And once the problem has been resolved
God has forgotten it so should we.

After you've walked this mile
You can still smile
God has forgiven us
So we must learn to forgive others.

Mistakes

95

It is normal to make mistakes
Taking the time to correct them
Is what it takes?
Admitting the truth for your own sake
Avoid any problem from becoming great.

Testimony

Thy testimony is a test
A trial you've stood and overcame
The storm that was in your life
God's hands reached out
To save, comfort, and delivered thy soul
From temptations and pitfalls
Ye shall boldly tell others your story
Because thy testimony is a sentimental praise
Glorify the Lord for the victory.

Thy testimony shall testify
God's word is pure, perfect, and true
The word shall compass and endure
From thence to evermore
The word converts the soul and
Transform the heart and mind of
Mankind who seeks Jesus Christ Whole hearted.

Thy testimony is a witness
When you stand still and pray
The blood of Jesus is pleading
And working on your behalf
The yoke of bondage is destroyed
Satan has to flee
Satan is defeated
The battle is won and
In Jesus you got the victory!

Peace

Peace is the comfort I find
Within my soul and mind
Peace is endurance with patience
Which I asked and God granted to me
My faith I can release with a certainty
And without a second thought
I don't have any doubts
Because my relationship with the Omnipotent
God is my innermost peace.

Peace is walking through green pasture
The harvest of God's garden
It is plentiful of herbs and fruits
Therefore the body feed on earthly nature
The soul seek God's word to fulfill the Spirit
My soul is delighted because
God promised to supply my every need
God gave to me contentment and peace.

Peace is rising above the mountains
Jesus is the giver of peace
Created all things in the universe
No one can escape nor hide
From the presence of God
The valley is very low
The mountain stand high
The arms of God stretch wide
To rescue you from the pitfall

The Creator who formed the foundation
Can meet you anywhere?
Jesus comes to forgive, deliver, and
Save you from the mountains in your life
Jesus is the giver of peace
Wants to see your face in peace
Upon His final return

A Time For Peace

Peace is the absence of war,
Nations acting an agreement to end hostilities
Families and friend reuniting
In a harmonious relation.

Peace is a time to be reborn
It is a state of reconciliation
Rebuilding our lives, our county and America's dream
America is a country of the free
For people like you and me.

We often regret the loss and sorrow
Of long endless wars
Memories of family members
I wished I still had
I realize this too will eventually pass
And peace will one day last.

Ecclesiastes 3:1

To every thing there is a season
And a time to every purpose under the sun.

A Family Reunion

A FAMILY REUNION IS A CELEBRATION
BRINGING OUR PEOPLE INTO A CLOSER
RELATION
AS WE COME FROM NEAR AND AFAR
SHARING KNOWLEDGE OF ROOTED HISTORY
IN OUR CONVERSATION, TALENT AND
PASSAGE STORY
OF A FAMILY TREE THAT BEGAN MANY
YEARS AGO

ALTHOUGH THE FAMILIES RESIDE
IN MANY STATES ON THE U.S. MAP,
THE REUNION BRIDGES US TO COME
TOGETHER
AND DO NOT ALLOW A GENERATION GAP.

OUR ANCESTORS WERE ACHIEVERS WITH
GREAT SUCCESS.
THEY STRIVED FOR THE VERY BEST,
AND DIDN'T SETTLED FOR NOTHING LESS
BUT OVERCAME ANY FEARS
THAT WOULD TRY TO CHASTEN AWAY THEIR
DREAMS.
THEY KEPT THEIR EYES AND MINDS
FOCUSING ON THE FINISHING PRIZE.

THEN ONE DAY THEY REALIZED
WHAT LEGENDENCY THEY MUST LEAVE
BEHIND,

TO KEEP OUR GENERATIONS AND
GENERATIONS
HOPE AND DREAMS ALIVE
AND THE FAMILY REUNION STRONG
AND CONTINUING TO GROW

BECAUSE OUR ANCESTORS HAD A
DETERMINATION
AND MUCH FAITH AND COURAGE
THEY BECAME POWERFUL LEADERS AND
GREAT PIONEERS.
THIS PASSED DOWN LEGENDENCY SHALL
NEVER END—WHY?
THUS, WE'RE ALL GIVING A FOUNDATION
AND FIRM BEGINNING.

A FAMILY REUNION THAT WAS BUILT
AND ROOTED LIKE A PLANTED TREE.

About the Author:

I am grateful to share poetry dealing with God's love, life's experiences, and spirituality. I pray and hope that each reader will be enlightened and encouraged in God's word. These words, my Savior and Lord, have placed on my heart and mind to write spiritual poems that will help to encourage, strengthen, and develop spiritual growth.

Since I have been writing spiritual poetry, I have established a closer relationship with my Heavenly Father. It is a wonderful feeling to experience the presence, love, joy and peace of God. Especially after my parents died, I have truly leaned and depend on God for guidance and directions in everything that I do.

I have earned a B.A. Degree in Business Administration, but most of importance, I have earned a B.A. Degree in Christ Jesus. With this Born Again Degree in Christ Jesus, I trust and believe that God is getting ready to elevate my talent to another level. As I am a blessing to others, I pray and ask that Jesus continue to bless me.

www.ingramcontent.com/pod-product-compliance
Lightning Source LLC
Chambersburg PA
CBHW031308060726
47590CB00003B/1111